SALT RUNS IN MY BLOOD

Also by Susan Schmidt

Song of Moving Water

Landfall on the Chesapeake, in the Wake of Captain John Smith

SALT RUNS IN MY BLOOD

Susan Schmidt

Kakapo Press
Beaufort, North Carolina
2015

Kakapo Press
susu@susanschmidt.net
www.susanschmidt.net

ISBN 13-978-0-9863835-0-2
ISBN 10-09863835-0-3

Cover photo is by Mark Hooper

Author photo is by Anne Smith Mahoney

Gratitude to

my sisters and

my godmothers

Tell me a story of deep delight.

—Robert Penn Warren, *Audubon: a Vision*

CONTENTS

I Estuary

II Open Ocean

III Pocket Water

IV Sea Level

I Estuary

Sunbright Both Burn

I crack my blinds at dawn
to see white or not
on brown lawn.
I want clean seasons, extremes.

I paint my house white inside
like a blanched Abaco beach
or Arctic glacial ice.
Sunbright both burn.
Will my heart melt?

Denali, pink at Solstice
like a conch shell,
looms high in sky and mind.
Snow birches call me north

but I am home where
I can name the trees:
Liriodendron tulipifera.
Dogwood lights the canopy
like sunshafts in a clearing.

White petals carpet southern
ground before Alaska thaws.

Friendly Fire

Who will love me as I love this land?
Shenandoah blue hills, Piedmont red clay,
Tidewater and Chesapeake.
Let us cross the river and rest in the shade.

When my father died, I could leave Virginia.
My father who taught me no other man was good
enough. When I do leave, I carry wounds from mother
and husband who claimed too loud to love me.

On tipsy midnight tours, my brother voiced Confederate
generals' dying words, named the seven hills of Richmond.
At twenty our father's father rolled the
Soldiers and Sailors Monument up Libby Hill.

On Monument Avenue, bees filled Lee's bronze horse
with honey. He died quietly as college president.
Jeb Stuart, on a dancing horse, died saying,
 "We must protect the ladies of Richmond."

In battle, Stonewall Jackson's own troops
shot him in the dark, thinking him enemy.
Dying, a week later, he said, "Come let us cross
this deep river and rest in the shade of the trees."

Landslide

I struggle to pull up a broken man,
both of us in rubber boots sinking deep,
sucked down in black water. In the morning
I know I will drown if I capsize my kayak
in the waters of the glacier.
I will drown in cold dark water.

A mile from the base of the glacier
on Prince William Sound
a voice booms bass, sinister,
"*Tebencof, Tebencof,*"
on the haunted path from the shore
to the Russian village gone a hundred years
abandoned by otter-trappers when the ice advanced.

The voice taunts, "*If you throw away the ring,
you won't drown*"—my star-ruby wedding ring.
"*No, the ring is my history. I can't cut out my scars.*"
Reaching Quaker clearness,
I finish the ritual: "*I divorce thee, Jack*"—
in my sleep, in my dream, in Alaska.

Terrified as I've ever been of the palpable curse,
to save myself, I invoke old ladies who love me,
"*Jean Potter, hold me in the Light.
Nancy Pierce, hold me in the Light,
Winifred Rashford, hold me in the Light*"—
Wide awake in the tent.

More afraid than when I rounded
the Twin Auk Bay headland into
the Gulf of Alaska in six-foot seas.

I leave the tent and pace
the gray-stone beach
until the sky brightens.

Not until I paddle out of the milky river
that flows from the toe of Tebencof Glacier,
not until I round Trinity Point into clear water—
am I free from being dragged under.

Salt Runs in My Blood

1

"Remember where you come from," Bus tells me.
Bus Conway, my neighbor down Indian Creek,
has peeled soft-shelled crabs for eighty years.
Bus gave me a fossil scallop shell he found
in the mud the size of an LP record.
Years ago he took a hunting buddy,
a museum man, to see a skull on a sandbar
where he set his crabtraps. In the clay bank
along the shore they found bodies curled
in fetal position and ceremonial brass bowls.
The first green of the golf course
covers the Algonkian burial ground.

2

Salt runs in my blood like an estuary.
My father's ancestors were captains
four hundred years on the Chesapeake.
Loading watermelons on a bugeye bound
for Baltimore, as a boy he would drop one,
grab a fistful of red, sweet heart-meat
and kick the rest off the dock. Eating just
the heart of watermelon was as rich
as I could imagine. Once his sailboat sank
off Stingray Point and he had to stay afloat
all night with jellyfish up his pantsleg.

3

At the bend in the road by meadows of wild mustard
past the unpainted shack with window-box flowers,
in the farmer's field along the rutted driveway
where Robert E. Lee's uncle was buried, I could
pick ears of corn without asking permission,
but I would thank the farmer in his yard full
of chickens and kittens. My father smoked bluefish
in the old refrigerator. He steamed trash cans
full of crabs that turned blue to red. Whoever
cranked the peach ice cream got to lick the paddle.

4

Every time I walk a dock I want to kneel
down to see the shine on the surface,
to see how deep the water is, whether
the bottom is sand or mud, grass or debris.
When I was five I leaned under the dock
at Fishing Bay to see what was swimming by
and my father scooped me up
when wasps swarmed in my face.

5

In pictures I always wear a bathing suit,
on a boat or a beach, happy to be wet.
When my father taught me to sail,
he yelled from shore to steer close to the wind
and lean on the high windward side.
I learned to balance these forces—
the sheet, the tiller, and my weight leaning back,
toes tucked under the rail. When I was not quick
enough in a gust to spill wind, the boat capsized.
I jumped on the centerboard to right the boat.

6

Sound spreads smooth under the plaster
vaulted ceiling of King Carter's chapel,
red brick church built in 1720.
The hymn comes from all directions
instead of the center at the intersecting naves.
Outside ladies pile cakes and casseroles
on tables in the loblolly grove. Gold
day-lilies border the lawn where my
father's grave marker lies flat,
set in the grass.

7

Last fall I walked into a farmhouse
that smelled like hot cinnamon
of a grandmother's cookies.
I felt then, "It's time to go home."

On the Chesapeake a homeplace
is a white clapboard house
on a point of land. I crouch
on the shore and look in lamp-lit
windows, still silhouette hidden
in the reeds, like the great blue heron
watching fish move at her feet.

Anadromous fish, I return
mature to shore to head upriver.
Flying ahead into the distance
is the heron. As I paddle
my boat, she flies the channel
around the next bend. She waits
until I float to her perch
in the pine tree, then lifts, cries,
and stretches her wings wide,
waiting ahead—the great blue.

8

In search of homeplace I sail my boat
across oceans but go aground in the creek
approaching the yacht club dock, grinding
halted on an oyster rock round the bend
from the house where my mother lives alone.
She's afraid when a sailboat heels over
in the wind, which is how sailboats move.

A deep-keeled ocean boat doesn't belong
up a shallow creek. It's cold, late and dark,
and she'll worry since she expects me by dusk.
But to row ashore I have to re-inflate the dinghy
stowed already for ocean passage, so I wait
for daylight and high tide to float off and
head down the Bay again to deep water.

In storm and in calm, sailing is continuous prayer.
As the wind vane steers through rough seas,
I lie in the bunk below, hoping my boat
won't break apart. My hand on the hull,
thin metal membrane, I sense my father's
palm meet mine. And I say to reassure him:
I'm fine, Daddy, you taught me to navigate.

Ink on My Fingers

Fiddlers, poets, tipplers, saints—
I didn't know Irish were low class
until my mother's best friend at eighty
told me, "My mother let me play with
your mother even though she was Irish."
A man on a bus to Kerry told me,
"Smith and Burke aren't Irish;
they've been here only a thousand years.
Now, Horan from Clonmel, that's Irish."

My great-grandfather sailed to Boston
before the famine, apprenticed to a printer,
bought the letterpress, died early, ink
on his fingers. Mother's other grandfather,
born too in Westmeath, planted the roses
in Hartford's Elizabeth Park, sifting soil
with his hands. Her father finished eighth
grade, was elected judge thirty years—
one generation after "Irish need not apply."

"Until I married your father and stopped
thinking," my mother told me, "I was
a journalist. You were born with ink
in your blood." Late at night, she pounded
the piano downstairs, just below my bed.
We choose where we are born, a Sufi mystic
told me, so sitting between my parents'
bicker and smoke at the dinner table,
I learned to reconcile opposites,
ink and salt in my blood.

Heidi, she had tried to name me,
mocking my father's surname.
At the house in the big city, Heidi
in the book saved soft white rolls
in her closet for her mountain grandfather
who baked dark whole-grain bread.
Months later, the rolls were hard as rocks.
Hungry middle of the night, I too want
to horde, afraid to be empty like my mother
who took Miltown with neat bourbon to sleep.

Sweet Tooth

My father's great-grandfather,
Poole's Island lighthouse keeper,
planted two hundred acres of peach trees.
Deep rich black soil more like Iowa, he said,
than anywhere on the Chesapeake.
Poole's Island Peaches were famous
sixty years until the Army took
our land for a bombing range.

My Daddy had a sweet tooth—
he loved a good ripe peach.
The summer after heart surgery,
when he had little will to live,
his eyes vacant just waking,
bedcovers to his chin, he spurned
my mother's cooking. So,
hungry and weak kneed,
he sliced himself sweet peaches.

At the river for a weekend, I fed him
what would taste good to me.
I chopped tomatoes, peppers, cucumber,
onion, garlic, parsley picked fresh—
steeped in V-8 juice for gazpacho, then
watched him dump in a cup of sugar.

My father's mother had baked Peach Kuchen—
raised yeast dough smothered with peach slices.
When I was just married, alone all day
in a southern-coast-town rental house,
after hand surgery, I sliced peaches and
kneaded dough one handed, so I could
bake Grandmother's peach cake
to taste anything familiar sweet.

Daughter

At twenty-one I dug through the barrel
of my mother's sewing remnants to piece
together a quilt. I took fine cotton lawn
of pastel field flowers, thin like silk,
costly cloth imported from London
that gave me value as a child.

They were scraps of Liberty Lawn
from dresses my mother had
smocked for me. She dressed me up
like a doll. I recall my vanity
in layers of crinolines,
hand-made flower-print dresses.

Retrieving my treasures stored
in an attic, I was sending boxes
down the stairs as my new husband
was packing the U-Haul truck.
He threw away, thinking it trash,
a black plastic bag of fabric.

Three years married, I nursed
my grudge of lost Liberty.
I picture the quilt I would have
made in tiny tentative stitches,
piecing memories with patches
of pink, yellow, and green,
one special-best blue Easter dress.

And as I sell the quilt in a dream yard sale
    give it away
I release grief over my lost child
    me as a little girl
and the daughter I won't have.

Table Rock

My father never yelled but used to tell
my mother, "Mary Anne, you're in irons,"
nautical talk meaning there was no wind
in her sails. I vowed no man would ever
belittle me. Good grades not good enough,
I paddled wild rivers, climbed rock cliffs.

The only girl at Outward Bound, I did
everything with the boys except run naked
and leap into the lake at dawn. Throwing
my weight for momentum, I fell off
the Ropes Course, shattered my wrist.
"Can you feel your fingers?" the sherpa
kept asking, driving to a clinic. Called
from golf, the bumptious country doctor
wore blue plaid pants, blinding-white shoes.

After catching a nine-hour ride, in pain
I did not let my mother bathe me, dirt
etched in my skin. If I hurt, she hurt worse.
When the Richmond doctor reset my wrist
set wrong, I let loose a blood-curdling yell
that blanched faces in the waiting room.

A month after my marriage, a UVA doctor
re-attached severed tendons. When
the cast came off, my new husband told me,
"Make it hurt," like a football coach.
It had hurt enough. The neighbor boys
rowed me across Taylors Creek, walked
me across Bird Shoal, so I could sweep
my new wrist through salt water.

Rappel

Could you keep your heart in wonder at the daily miracles in
your life, your pain would not seem less wondrous than your joy.
                                        Kahil Gibran

To work in the forest for a summer
I had to take three shots against the disease
carried by brown ticks that hang on bushes
waiting for warm blood to walk by.
I got sick forty-eight hours each time,
laid low and too sore to lift an ax.
Doctors know now the serum is more risk
than the chance of spotted fever.

Fort Valley has always been a safe place.
George Washington would have sheltered
here if Cornwallis had won at Yorktown.
When the Shenandoah Valley was burned
in the Civil War, Stonewall Jackson
hid the Home Guard in The Fort till he
swooped down on Union troops, and
they didn't know where he'd come from.

Once in a sundown rain squall
returning trailwork shovels, I sheltered
in the warehouse waiting out the storm,
weighted by the inhibition of men
not swapping dirty stories
with one woman among them.

On my days off building fish dams,
digging firebreaks, I milked
the ranger's goats on his perfect farm
with apple orchard, wife and sons.
In noon shade I dozed on a moss bed
up the trail past the rock where
the granddaddy rattler basked.
I stepped over snakes ignoring fears
my mother fed me. I knew someone would
come looking if I wasn't back by dark.

In Passage Creek behind my cabin
I collected blue stones like Indian turquoise,
slag from Iron Furnaces a father named for
three daughters: Catherine, Elizabeth, Caroline.
I scaled the stone tower of Catherine Furnace
to teach rappelling, climbing a rope and sliding down.
I taught wilderness survival skills to city kids
who missed street drugs. Me naïve, I watched
one girl hold open a paper bag for another
to hyperventilate, withdrawing from heroin
at sixteen. The ranger refused to send her home.

Oblivious to teenagers having sex in the woods,
on my dulcimer I painted wild strawberries,
sang "Shady Grove" and "Shenandoah."
To learn mountain women's work I spun
oily wool from black sheep that graze
by the Shenandoah River's seven bends.
Indigo flowers—that dye cloth blue—are
yellow. Where the creek spread into a bog,
I picked cress, brewed sweet tea
from feather-fingered pennyroyal.

Wary of bear in the same thorned thicket,
I picked four quarts of blackberries to make wine—
sifting boiled berry juice through a window screen,
added baker's yeast and sugar. Since
King's Crossing General Store had no balloons,
a neighbor, observing my industry, volunteered from
his glove compartment, to seal the neck of the jug
fermenting dark in my closet, an expandable
vapor barrier—which stood erect the fourth day
and withered to produce sour liquor.

After the summer crew's last dinner,
the forest ranger, whose orchard and family
I coveted, drove me back to the trailer.
The first night the student bunks were empty,
I woke with my boss ready to rape me.

Do I Dare?

Peach trees do not resist southern pests
that plague them, so die sooner than apples
on the same south-facing slope. As winters

alternate weeks of freeze and thaw, as
the weather in our world goes wonky,
late frosts kill peach blossoms that bud

early. Peaches from the grocery store
rot before they ripen. From a farm stand
is the only way to buy them. At the

Farmers Market south of Asheville
a boy cups a peach in his facing
palms, his fingers rip it apart.

"Here, taste this," he says, handing me one
dripping half—luscious, creamy yellow.
"Taste this one"—salmon-pink. I buy

a bushel from the boy, and the next night
blanch, peel, pit, slice and slip
ripe peaches into jars to pressure-cook.

A bushel is too much for one person
to process in one night. After working
for the Forest Service a summer in

Fort Valley, I came home with a bushel
of apples and a bushel of peaches. For a day
I stood next to my mother in her kitchen,

the best thing we ever did together—washing,
slicing, stewing fruit, baking pies, stirring
the Foley Food Mill that sieves out seeds

and skins for smooth apple sauce.
I did not tell my mother my recent grief.
I learned young she never kept my secrets.

Sandy Loam

My first imprinted landscape—
smooth rolling fields
crossing each bridge—
Pamunkey, Mattaponi,
Rappahannock—
along Route 360 to the river cottage.

Here on his farm, Edmund Ruffin
crushed marl so soil could
take up nitrogen from dead fish
or manure after settlers' tobacco
depleted sandy loam by these
rivers where Indians grew corn.

Down the river I covet
a blueberry farm for sale,
conjuring pie and jam and
morning yoga with a breeze,
but the buildings all need repair
and I'm no carpenter.

At dusk I leave
the dream-yarn homeplace
turn east and drive
a mile or so
in double west-bound lanes:
The approaching pickup honks,
        its headlights flash:
"Hey girl," the guy yells
out his window, "You're
headed the wrong way."

No joke, my first response.
I've been looking a long time for the right direction.

Equilibrate

1
I was happy alone in the mountains
in the middle of a hundred acres
with a mile-long dirt driveway,
with hardwood trees and topsoil.
But I marry an oceanographer
who thinks he is Jacques Cousteau.
Lonelier married, I mourn
the loss of green and shade.

On Bird Shoal's vast beige
flatness, I find the green film
of algae on sand at low tide.
I trace sandpiper tracks,
ghostcrab calligraphy,
collect purple wampum shells.

At Shackleford, Jacques leads me
over dune fields to the beach.
The air is still except for the buzz
of insects. I pick off sand spurs
stuck in my feet and seed ticks
crawling up my legs. I'm hot
with no water to quench my thirst.
Salt water burns my eyes, sand
grates my sun-burned skin.
Preferring privacy, I refuse
when he wants sex in the dunes.

2

When Jacques's science buddies visit from upstate,
he takes us to dive on a ship wrecked off
Bogue Banks. We have to share gear
so he takes all of them down first
as I ride the sea swell alone in the boat
with no shade— finally facing that
Jacques sleeps with girls in his lab.
When the guys roll back over the sides,
dripping wet, refreshed, sputtering
about all the fish they've seen,
I want to dive down too.

Jacques rigs me in black rubber,
an airtank and mouthpiece,
borrowed mask and fins,
a man's weight belt. I jump
over first and overweighted
I sink deep and fast.
In the murky water
I cannot tell up from down
nor how long I am submerged,
full of lethargy and longing.
I'm profoundly disappointed
there are no neon reef fish here.

My air will not last, so
I kick toward the green light
in the direction I hope is up.
I know only not to hold
my breath, blowing bubbles
until I break the surface.
Jacques says he couldn't clear his nose,
equalize pressure
to come as deep as I was.
It's hard to come back
from diving too deep.

There is always
this distance between us,
the plate glass I shatter
when I rise from water to air.

3
I am safe when I sail alone
unafraid I'll run aground,
be surprised by storm
or becalmed before dark.
Before I leave Jacques for good,
I sail to Lookout to catch bluefish for bait,
like magic, so easy to cast
and catch them. In the surf
I see the wings of cownose rays
slicing the wall of water.
Flying fish skim above the surface,
escaping predators.

At the eight-mile buoy off the Cape
where the Gulf Stream veers in close
I beat the water with a boat hook
to call in amberjack. They gather
excited, the size of sheep,
eager as brides to be caught,
changing colors—yellow,
blue-green, iridescent.

I hook one right away and reel in
twenty minutes, straining the rod
with the weight, recalling, "Keep the tip up."
I can hardly lift the eighty-pound fish
to clip the hook. But caught,
it has lost all color. Giving the fish
its freedom gives me courage.

II Open Ocean

Weather Helm

When I leave the marriage
Rosalie takes me sailing
out the inlet to open ocean

in her Herreschoff-28
classic wood sloop
with a heavy keel

Trim the sails right
and the boat will hold its course
though I have forgotten how

to feel the wind on my face
to sense wind direction
to see the stars

When Rosalie tells me
to take the helm, to steer,
I am afraid to capsize

I can't right
an ocean boat
by jumping on its hull

but I touch the tiller
as the boat heels
perfectly balanced

The Watery Part of the World

On land I was crushed by foreboding,
Apprehensive to leave the dock
Shorthanded, worn rigging, weak engine.
I can make no clear choice on land.

We start with good weather predictions.
Jumping off there's no turning back.
Crossing the Gulf Stream we watch ships pass
Three smooth days then the wind picks up.

I sail 'cross the ocean mid-winter
Delivering a rich man's yacht,
An ultralight racer from Fastnet.
Triple-reefed, we surf at eight knots.

Ten days we are driven to weather.
Winds thirty-five, forty-five, more.
High seas sweep the deck, fill the cockpit.
Each fifth wave cascades down my neck.

With no moon under darkest of skies,
Zooplankton glow phosphorescent
In the wave that buries the lee rail.
Through high seas we plunge, pound, and veer.

Strong gust: the wind vane jumps off its track.
"Bring her down, every second counts."
The mainsail blows out when we broach.
We jibe wildly, drop the sail.

We fall in our bunks in wet raingear
Always ready to work up on deck.
For two weeks we take turns sleeping.
No sun sights, the SatNav won't track.

The forestay breaks, the mast shivers.
The jib halyard pops, the jib rips. Lines
Chafe through and worn shackles fly loose.
My crew works on foredeck unharnessed.

I ask the wind to drop ten knots—
Anticipate sighting land.
I give my strength to the rudder and keel—
I know I'm where I should be.

Topside on night watch every evening
I dread the horizon's dark clouds.
So I clear my voice singing carols—
My voice clears the sky for the stars.

I keep company with Sirius, Aldebaran.
The three stars of Orion's belt roll
Over my sky east to west. The moon
Shines my path south-south-east.

I'm the only one awake for miles.
Considering my fate and my planet,
I vigil for peace oceans and species—
This moment of calm, thirty knots.

In the clear sky and empty mid-ocean,
Though storm clouds loom soon ahead,
And wailing winds drown out my small
voice, I sing loud and know I am heard.

The clouds clear overhead while I sing.
In the sky Mars passes Jupiter.
Winds blow hard, but I steer on course.
My small ship is safe in God's hands.

Not confident of our position shot by a
Warped plastic sextant, we swing wide
Of Anegada, approach Antigua from the east.
The last stormy night is the longest.

A strange beacon light warns of reefs.
As we anchor, I dance on deck to reggae
From shore. Before I swim to touch land,
A harbor dawn-downpour rainbow.

Abaco

I lean my back against each oar stroke,
sprinting to round the point of land
as the Bahama sun goes down. The globe
bulges ellipsoid, yolk-red, before it drops,
resisting the pull underwater. I wait—
unblinking—and miss the green flash again.
Below the horizon the sun pastels cloud wisps,
like the Hopetown beach of crushed conch shells.

I hear tell I can induce the green flash
by squinting, or split-second blinking.
It appears only to a mystic few,
facing west, as the sun sets over water.

I first saw a sun set over water
trailing my father as he collected shells
on Sanibel. On Mykonos with a college boy
I watched the sun set then the moon rise
in the stone-arched window, too drunk
on retsina to lose our virginity.

Make My Heart Sing

My heart leaps when my spaniel's
long ears rise as she bounds
in high grass to scout a rabbit's path
and see bees pollinating.
I lift my arms, as if wings,
to fill my lungs.

I say "wait" each day so she'll stop
on command when running the beach.
Her lifespan is short,
like my own, on another scale.

Inside she'll rub a mud streak
on the white slipcover,
which I can wash.
I bought a white sofa
before the brown dog.

Her footpads smell
musty like humus.
More alive if she swims
daily, she leaps to retrieve
a stick in the creek.
In the Gaelic myth, she's
a seal who moved ashore.
Silkie like me, happiest wet.

20 Shades of Purple

Long lean Dale in Fairbanks worked
six months a year in Antarctica
welding pipes to drill cores two thousand
feet deep. When I cooked dinner for fourteen
at Hidden Hill, my turn once a week,
with three gallons of ice cream—
at the table waiting, Dale would read
compression tables for Caterpillar bulldozers.
In the dozen pockets of his worn Carhartts
he carried tools to repair most anything.
When I ordered a plum rain suit—
Dale said he knew only one purple.

"Shades and hues of red and blue," I said.
"Fruit, flowers, and gems. There's violet,
iris, periwinkle, lavender that sound like
they smell and taste. Wait." I ran for my
thesaurus. "Not just plum, but damson,
prune, and raisin. Look at the Aurora Borealis.
There's amethyst, eggplant, magenta, mulberry."

Laconic Dale shook his head.
He couldn't see but one color purple.

On a Carolina beach twenty-some years
later, an ancient barnacle is fuchsia.
The sunray-venus is mauve plaid.
The tiny coquina is lilac.
Between ridges of an oyster is grape.
Inside an olive shell looks like
blackberry stain on white linen.
Shards of surf clam, once strung like coins
as Indian wampum, how I measure
my wealth, cover the whole spectrum
—hyacinth to heliotrope.

Lift Me Up

The college pond froze the week
before Christmas in sixth grade
and I walked a mile to skate.
In the middle of the pond
I fell through thin ice
up to my armpits. But
no one noticed. "Klutz,"
I thought to myself.
Flailing my arms I wriggled
from the water until I could
stand safely and glide to shore.
A friend's mother drove me
home, wet, to an empty house.

Between sailing jobs,
first night I slept in my house
three years after divorce,
one wet drip hit my nose.
Checking the roof leak,
I fell through the ceiling
knee deep
when I stepped off
a joist in the attic.
Same feeling:
who will lift me up?

Sleeping Naked

in the first fall chill
before winter freezes the pipes
in the summer cottage by the bay
before daylight
an explosion lifts me
from my mattress

I pull on jeans and sweatshirt
and run across the lawn
to the creek
where my neighbor's
40-foot workboat blazes in flames
reflected red on the water

I plunge in
and pull two young men
to the shore
blown clear by the blast
stunned but
cursing a blue streak

the waterman
is driving his wife
to a doctor this morning
his nephews turned on
the gasoline engine
without venting fumes in the bilge

folks in Glass wake
to watch his boat burn
to the waterline and sink uninsured
in the dawning shadow
the two boys find me,
wet, and apologize

Rappahannock

Walking down the long hill
I greet my father's bones that
lie in the river, not his skeleton
but once-bright spars of wooden boats
he sailed and sank. On the beach
my water spaniel splashes shallows,
chasing ducks she'll never catch.

At my feet I scout glints on the sand,
blue-green glass with smooth edges.
Sea glass is my wage this year, what
I carry away, sorry not so much to lose
the job in this lousy economy but
to leave again where my father raised me.

When the stock market crashed,
at twenty he left his father's house
on Piscataway Creek and restored
a fifty-foot wooden schooner
he called *Black Duck*. He sailed
the Rappahannock
          and the Chesapeake
instead of finishing college.

My brother across the river
wants to name his new sloop
after a seven-syllable Italian opera
that no waterman can pronounce
or remember if he radios for help.
But he names it for our father's boat,
orders matching hats, and one
for his daughter, *Black Duckling*.

The water is glass flat, just right
for rowing. I lift my eyes
to the sky and horizon
dawn or dusk rose-glow, ripple or chop.
I look northeast to Carters Creek
        sad to leave where folks know my family,
northwest to Greenvale Creek
        to move from the rivers my father sailed,
west to Piscataway past the misty timber headland.

Prothonotary Warbler

World birder, Dusti has flown
from Ecuador to see her dying father.
I drive kayaks two hours to share
swamp birds of Carolina.
"Smells like home," she says.

End of March is early for migrants
but the weather's warming early
so chicks and the bugs they eat
are all out of sync.

Keen, we round each bend
of the creek, high water—
river birch, cypress, willow oak,
sweet gum, and there—bright

lemon breast, darting and dancing
on limbs—swamp canary and
her male, yellow orange, robed
in citrus like Roman clerks.

Carry Me Down

More than any teacher's words
from high school
I remember in my bones
the rhythm of "Stand by Me."

My head under water
in the tub I can hear
just the bass line
of rock and roll on the radio.

In college I dated the Whiffenpoof
bass singer who showed me what
fish say, pushing fingers into
his cheeks, "Peach pie, peach pie."

Treading water
after surgery to fix the knee
I tore skiing the glades forty
years ago when the bass man split

I hum along
buh bum bum- bump
buh bum bump- buh
buh buh bump- bum.

I fired the dour surgeon for telling
me, You will feel more pain.
Your expectations are too high
to be active at this age.

Instead, I wore a black brace
when I climbed Mt Aspiring
in case my knee collapsed so
no one had to carry me down.

No Place Else on Earth

In the Southern Alps glaciers are melting.
Under the world's largest ozone hole
on South Island, a five-inch scar mars
the captain's cheek on Milford Sound.
I mumble, "Knife fight?" and he grins.
When I say, "Melanoma?" he nods.
When Pacific islands flood, refugees
of sea-level rise will clamber
for New Zealand's peaks.

But the mountain spine is twisting, wrung
like a wet towel. Ten thousand tremors
in Christchurch spilled books and dishes
from shelves. Three major quakes shook down
the Cathedral tower and condemned the nave,
where I had watched ballet dancers in skimpy
flower costumes raise funds for choir boys
to sing in Britain. The cathedral dean,
Peter Beck, silly and mischievous, rocked
down the aisle robed as Jack in the Pulpit.

Climate change matters more on an island.
Half my life ago I would have stayed
in these mountains by Milford Sound—
transcendent landscape—loved by someone
with a true heart for no more than who I am.
I would have left the States and a bad marriage.
But, after my father's death, who
would care for my mother?

Thirty years ago, on steep wet Milford Track
I may have seen a kakapo, nocturnal ground-
nesting parrot, moss-green camouflage with
sharp curved bill and jolly jowls like an owl,
heard the male's *boom-boom* across a chasm.
They have chicks only every five years,
and the tree whose fruit makes them randy
is dying too. Now, a hundred kakapos
stay alive in a preserve off Stewart.

Half my life later, trekking South Island,
as the bus bores through long tunnels,
drops ten thousand feet to sea level,
a dozen dizzy switchbacks to Milford Sound,
for two days I live in two times at once.
Then and now, me young still a chance and
me old too late to move, though few regrets.

On the tourist boat I do not sleep
but all night on deck savor
what my life might have been.
I would help my Kiwi man and sons
grow Merino sheep and Sauvignon Blanc.

At dawn, rain-cloud mists lift and
sun spins rainbows on waterfalls
plunging from sharp granite peaks
reflected on the silver-black fjord.
Every kind of rare species comes
to play—fur seals, dusky dolphins,
crested penguins with yellow eyebrows.
I jump in glacier-cold water
and pop up fast,
no place else on earth this clean.

Such Grace

At dusk
black-capped, sharp-winged
least terns weave lace,
dart and turn like bobbins,
grazing no-see-ums
that bite tender skin on my wrists.

Terns nest on the beach spit
south of Deep Creek
a foot or two from high tide.
A nest is shallow like my palm,
the egg camouflaged
the color of sand.

Having rowed hard
against wind and tide,
I drift down the creek,
free ride, pushed home
by tide and wind,
back to the landing.

As I watch the sun drop west,
curved-bill ibis,
black-legged egrets
wing east down Taylors Creek
to roost before dark.

III Pocket Water

Food Chain

When asked why
        he looked so young,
the Dalai Lama's doctor said,
        "Eat well and drink well
and don't get eaten."

In the rainforest
        a hunter up a tree
mimics bird song to set a trap.
        Hearing prey, a panther
stalks the man for dinner.

Dull-color birds like geese
        are monogamous, share childcare,
live longer than more colorful males.
        But beware
if pale male birds or fish,
        men with gray skin,
are ill or listless.

The flashiest male of the species
        attracts more mates.
Yet, for fish, color lures predators
        as well as a lady.
To live longer, he should limit
        his time exposed
swimming in bright light.

Dear Robert Penn Warren,

We sat next to each other on an airplane in 1975
from Richmond to LaGuardia. I had required my
high-school juniors to attend your lecture the night
before, but they couldn't understand a word you said.

Your daughter had survived an airplane crash in Rome
sitting in the row where the plane cracked in half.
Your wife had won a prize for her book about
growing oyster spat on plates in Brittany.

You said no word of your own books, but told stories—
Hemingway really was a bully. Sparring in Paris, when
the bout was over, Fitzgerald put on his eyeglasses.
The big guy threw one last punch and broke them.

When James Agee arrived for a party with a wife and baby,
backseat full of dirty diapers, "Ah, the Agee-an Stable,"
you laughed a hearty red-faced laugh. My student, learning
style, had told me Jimmy Carter spoke like Agee wrote.

In New York, we walked, you and I, by baggage claim where
twenty minutes later a terrorist bomb killed eleven people.
We rode the limousine to New Haven where I was
visiting a guy at Yale I adored, who thought me just a pal.

Tom was best at what I want to do. Is love just projection?
We had met at Andover and then Oxford. Before my flight, we
walked all night across London: he pulled roses out of a
dustbin.
We felt the boom when an IRA bomb blew up a car a block
away.

Red Warren, once your hair was red. The year you died, I studied your essays to pass PhD exams. Jim Dickey read your Audubon poem at his wife's grave. "Tell me a story. In this century, and moment, of mania." Bombs we walked by and survived.

"Tell me a story of deep delight." He wasted his last years writing novels for money. Before he died, gaunt Dickey jamming on guitar, me on bass, my Georgia boyfriend on fiddle mouthed, "You mean Dickey from *Deliverance*?"

I Wade Rivers as Prayer

I wade rivers as prayer, immersed in flow and shine,
scramble steep stone slides, skirt deep pools
overhung by hemlock, fringed by ferns. I turn over
rocks to see how soon insect larvae will emerge.
Fish suspend mid depth, mid stream until flies
rise, birthing from the bottom, or sink ephemeral.

After two weeks of rain no fish are biting,
the Chattooga is muddy and the bottom
half-sand from erosion upriver. I roll-cast
into white froth below the falls. The woolly
bugger drifts, weighted, underwater, until it
snags: a rock, I think. I gather looped line,
jiggle, twitch, and cannot retrieve.

Then your massive tail flicks—and awe.
I keep my rod tip up, steady my feet
in the sand. You do not budge. When you
surface, I yell, "Holy Mother." I could never
have imagined your size, long and thick
as a thigh. I let you run since I can't stop
you, till you swim docile to my feet.

I want to embrace you—luck, gift, blessing—
Brown trout longer than my widest stance,
but you break the leader when I reach
to pluck the hook from your lip.

Big trout, I want to know what you have learned
in the dark pool, holding in the current,
brooding under rhododendron. You are wise
to survive this long. You remember pristine
when headwaters were wild. I sit by your pool,
watch the hatch of blond caddis in late
oblique light, past dusk wait for you to rise.

Early Fruit

"Clip to one central leader and a scaffold
of four or five branches so light enters
the center of the tree. Prune any branch
with a steep angle. You can make no mistake."

These trees will bear early fruit for camp kids
to pick apples for cider, applesauce, jam,
and pie. "Remove first-year fruit so the tree
grows roots," the extension agent told me.

We walk his orchard together, a man I fancy
and his daughters of two divorces. I'm shy;
they smile, blond like sunshine. We pinch
leaf-green aphids, flick off June bugs.

Wearing straw hats, we girls sing "Lamsy dotes
and dozy dotes" and "Oh what a beautiful
morning" in the coming rain. I oppose
pesticide; no matter, he'll spray.

With trees, I can guide how they grow.
Though I'd like to think I'm ready to tend needy
step-daughters, when they tire and whine, I won't
stop pruning all the young trees I watered by hand.

Deep Pool

No one will love Darcy as I do
for his grace when he wades, swift
over slippery rocks, fluid on felt soles.
He doesn't cast long but drops
the fly over a rock to a hidden pool;
he who hesitates unsure on shore
is confident in a stream.
Every other cast catches a trout.

I am like no other woman
he has ever met.
On Carolina pocket water
we wade the river tunnel, tandem.
We share this: wet feet
fly-hatch in green leaf-light
joy at trout leap
cataract and calm.

Intent on trout, I don't watch the sky
darken early, a front whipping up
the escarpment. Darcy who fears lightning
insists we stop fishing. He could not
have contrived the storm
would drive us to shelter.

The tin roof slopes too low to stand.
The air is mist, one drip strikes the floor.
We shuck neoprene waders, share my
apple and cheese, recline on winter leaves
inside the wind and walls of water.

Outside is other light, other time.
Darcy says, "Your heart is a deep pool."
I say, "I thought my heart was a fish."
"No," he says, "your heart is a deep pool."

Puer Eternis

At the end of summer
Darcy leads us off the trail
where yellow stakes flag a nest,
yellow jackets stringing up
from a hole in the dirt.
Our feet pound the earth like
a drum. In the drought at camp
on every hike a kid was stung.
Sunscreen sweats into my eyes.
Darcy pays me no mind.

We balance on mossy rocks
across a stream, steep and slick,
past Uncle's Creek Falls.
I do not break stride but keep up,
third in line, behind his daughter.
Darcy inherited three thousand acres
that I roamed five years as my own.
By a remote trout stream at Easter
bloomed two hundred yellow ladyslippers
in a dell likely few have ever seen.

We pass a meadow feed-plot and follow
the trace of a century-old lumber road.
A hunter has marked the place again.
At a plastic bag tied to a bush we turn
down a wash to terraced ground
facing south. Settlers always built
close to a spring. They walked a gap
up the hill called the Blue Wall.

No one has been here in two hundred years
except deer poachers. Bushwhacking at sixteen
Darcy found the lost chimney once himself.
With his magnet Darcy finds no nails.

Logs were notched, stacked, dovetailed,
chinked around 1790. Rubble of stones
is all that's left, wood long rotted.

Raindrops spatter our faces and
we shelter under hard holly leaves.
Darcy spreads his parka over blond
Catherine and his own shoulders
like a bird's big wings.
Summer has been so dry
I forgot my own raincoat.

When the sky clears, we range about.
I hope for pottery shards, a pewter spoon,
the wife's iris bulbs—to picture her life
in this place I wanted to live. Up this hill
above the waterfall, I believe, are native
brook trout. How much is believing
worth to me? Scraping for metal,
Darcy talks about a geologic fault,
the rift between us irreparable.

On a different path straight downhill are
two red efts the size of my baby finger,
orange salamanders with gray dots.
Lime-green fungus on a downed tree.
We cross turkey scratch, musk scent,
blundering-black-bear torn leaves.
I lag behind. Leaving Darcy,
I'll leave his land. From the shade
a yearling deer holds my gaze
until I break free.

At the bottom of the hill
by the fence of a hay meadow all mown,
goldfinches bob on top of thistles,
half a dozen in full sun.

Rosa Chinensis Mutabilis

1
The guard chides
when I poke my nose
above the rope barrier
at the Monet show.

In Giverny, near
the din of artillery
at the Somme he built
a pond to copy its

palette of poppies,
water lilies, and water
as blurs and brush
strokes on canvas.

I recompose
his landscape
standing at a distance
instead of up close.

2
Godmother Nancy,
Garden Club judge, told me,
"You must weed, prune, fertilize,
mulch, pinch off old flowers."

I dabble in dirt for color
to attract butterflies and birds
not for how the garden
looks but how I feel.

Yet, first thing when
I come home in the dark
from working away
is deadhead the China rose.

With enough rain it blooms
spring to Christmas—honey-
yellow, watermelon, copper-
pink, and finally magenta.

Small Point

The porch on the cliff overlooks a vast
sand flat, a lighthouse on a rock island.
The tidal river fills a broad marsh at high tide
and empties twice a day. High tide, low tide,
sun and fog. The full moon shines on wet sand,
full three nights, and pulls the tides higher
and lower. I no longer like King Canute
command the tide to stop, or like
Matthew Arnold expect much love.

I walk the sand road through spruce woods
past a beaver-pond and ramble the rock point
in a cloud. As fog lifts, a skiff bobs beyond
the surf, two rods bending, a father and child
catching striped bass, and a guide unhooking fish,
one hand on the wheel pointing the boat to sea.
My father died before we had fished enough.
At night, the surf roars out the window.
The sea and moon fill my room's white walls.

Below the inn at dawn mid-tide I wade
the channel thigh deep, no sunrise
in the fog. The beach stretches empty
four miles. When I reach a rock outcrop
I see a distant figure wading a sandbar where
surf breaks. He moves his feet precariously.
Reticent, I recognize a person like me
who likes to enter the elements. If I blink
he may disappear, obscured in fog or swept
to sea. The man on the shoal bends each
forearm at an angle of prayer. I am moved,

myself reverent. I would wade to him
if I did not fear I'd intrude. Before I turn
back to blueberry pancakes and the flight
south, his arms fling forward a surf rod
invisible to me to cast for stripers
streaming past the coast.

Wild Sister

At FAO Schwartz in New York
when I was four, I wanted the
life-size Steiff tiger. My Daddy
told me he'd buy it if I could
carry it out the door. I tried,
couldn't lift it, and cried.

Christmas before dawn
my brother snuck down,
shined a flashlight
under the tree, came back
for me, and we tiptoed the stairs.

In the dark two green glass
eyes blazed bright, quite
alive. I ran back to bed
until daylight. Under the tree
I found a tiger my size.

My Steiff tiger is the first thing
I'll carry out, with my dog,
if the house is burning down.
"Wild sister" and "best friend"
I whisper, then release her.

Eyes and Glass

Glory be to God for dappled things
Gerard Manley Hopkins

My bare feet and felt soles
of my boots shine with mica dust.
In drought I do not cast for trout
suffocating in low pools but wade
upstream and watch the water.
Minding the light is how Quakers pay attention.
Mountain laurel rings Celo Meeting,
converted goat shed by the river.
Singing children and silence
shelter me up the hill from a violent
country that ignores a decade at war.

In the borrowed house I push hand-blown
glass-art to the back of a shelf, one-of-a-kind
Jack-in-the-Pulpit vase, but absent-minded
knock from the counter the only store-bought
glass in the kitchen—a Pyrex cup-measure
shatters on the tile floor. Shards shatter and slide.
Broken glass trains my eye to see what shines.
I sweep and wet-wipe the last ice glints
so no glass sliver will stick in my skin.

Three thousand feet above sea level,
glass walls face west. Celo Knob, twice as high
across South Toe Valley, keeps me company,
cloud or fog, blue sky or starlit. One moment
when I turn, a bird thunks the glass, drops
to the deck, still warm in my palm, a speck
of blood on her feather-down white breast.
I lay the gnatcatcher in the notch
of a tree to decompose with dignity.

At the edge of my eye
     a flash of *falling firecoal.*
In soft rain a leaf catches
a shaft of sunlight. I check—
only one yellow leaf on the deck
and not a flame.
In a rhododendron tunnel I walk
the grassy path to a memorial
for a grieving young man's wife.
I place the gilt leaf in my pocket
on ashes of the fire circle—
the charm of some such thing
dead early out of season.

Sunday noon after Quaker Meeting
I slip down a steep bank on the South Toe
to a secret swimming hole dammed deep
behind a riffle where the river bends.
I stroke against the current then float back
by rainbow trout the color of water
     rose moles astipple down their flanks.
Sunlit wet rocks blaze gold.
The only thing I really own is light on the water.

Underwater I grasp a fist-hunk of mica.
I heft this rock
     like holding my heart in my hand
and layer by layer peel
clear sheets of isinglass
    infinitely thin
until I reach a pure core.

Mirabile Dictu

Inside I feel the pull of tides—incoming, outgoing
—like the periwinkle snail that climbs Spartina
on each tide cycle. Deadlines on my desk;
eschew excuses: The sky is blue.

With lucky timing, wind and tide at my back
push me paddling six miles around Carrot Island
to look for the wee rare red-knot. Overhead
wheeling gulls and terns, pelicans in formation.

The tidal current streams east out Taylors Creek.
Sunday morning no motorboat wake. On the shore,
Louisiana heron, a burnished osprey on a bush.
Slack high at Lennoxville Point's eroding bank.

Kingfishers chitter from down-tree branches.
Northeast breeze blows me out North River into
the sound by copper-green Middle Marsh to island
hammocks where white ibis and egrets stand sentinel.

Abnormally high tide, so I can float over mudflat
channels usually dry, because Arctic ice melt
slows the Gulf Stream flowing north by Iceland
—so the Sargasso Sea, offshore, slumps a bit.

Four inches of rain in one day flooded Front Street.
The worst year ever for pollen, mosquitoes, fleas.
Hottest October on record, ocean still 76 degrees.
But don't fret sea level. Today, see abundance:

Summer plovers and sandpipers still here, winter birds
arriving. On a beach spit, watch fall migrants: among still
whimbrels, willets—two gamboling godwits on their way
to Patagonia, whose long bills curve upward toward God.

IV Sea Level

After the Virginia Tech Shooting

Walking the Camino
four hundred miles step by step
all month Ben and I
heard a man had died
climbing the Pyrenees
from St Jean to Roncesvalles.

News passed in a hundred
languages, shoulders shrugged
by yellow shell-shaped signs.
Was it a heart attack? Crossing
the Meseta, hot dry high plain, we
could understand heat exhaustion.

One pilgrim said, "I was
on the mountain
in the blizzard that day."

The young man dead
was a stockbroker, cocky,
bold, who pressed on alone
in a white-out, lost the path,
and froze—when others
hunkered down with strangers
who had enough fear to stop.

Swimming in a Meteor Shower

1
Three of us in the truck cab,
a tall young black man
in the middle and his brother
driving. To move to the coast
again, I hired him
to load furniture and drive
the U-Haul across the state.
Late at night, suddenly he demands,
"I need cash now." Starting
to freak, he thrashes, "Things are
going to take a bad turn. Pull off.
We're going to leave her by the side
of the road and sell her stuff."
Or worse.

What can I say to a guy in drug-withdrawal?
Every Quaker asks herself how she'll respond
to violence. When he conks out,
the empty stretch Kinston to New Bern,
I cringe against the door ready to leap,
truck going sixty-five.

At the airport, I jump out
and ask a cop for help who tells me,
"Pay the boys and be done."
Alone the last hour, driving
the 36-foot truck by myself
with an empty tank
he didn't fill at the gas stop,
I feel numb terror. In the morning
new students help unload my piano,
sofas, and sixty boxes of books, not yet
aware of burning towers on TV.

For the next month I am scared
a strange plane will come
from the horizon over the sea.

2
Early October in Beaufort
the first cold wind is called the mullet blow
when fish born in marshes swim out the inlet
for two years at sea. Wading birds, surf-rods,
and gill nets wait to catch the rush of fish.

I avoid swimming when sharks feed at dusk
and dawn. The water at Radio Island
is cleaner at incoming tide—shrimp docks
and live-aboard boats upstream. I wade in,
immerse, float, stroke, and
turn my neck to breathe. Suddenly
I'm swimming into light
like a meteor shower.
Inch-long silversides stream around me,
silver stripes painted on clear bodies.
I feel safe, luminous, but stand thigh deep
when I remember bluefish
with sharp teeth chase smaller fry.

In the sky: hundreds of black skimmers
roll in a wave like shaking dust
from a quilt. I figure they undulate
for fun after eating their fill of fish.
As they bank in synchrony
their color changes—
black backs, white bellies and
underwings catch the light.

Dwell in Safety

My town juts into the ocean twenty miles
from the Gulf Stream. Why do you live
willingly in the path of hurricanes?
someone upstate asked. I say with faith—
No place is safer than the beach to face wind
and water, because high tide ebbs back to sea.

Isabel approached the coast blowing 150 miles
an hour, which would have knocked Beaufort flat,
        force growing exponentially with speed.
As the barometer dropped, I hauled the boat
from the dock, moved porch chairs to the shed.
Heart-sick I said, "Not here. Hit someplace else, please."

The scary part is waiting. Afraid to be stranded
on a highway, I stayed put alone in my dark house,
plywood boarding windows. Nine feet above sea level
ants marched inside as water rose a block away.
At the eye at the depth of low pressure,
my ribs and wrist ached—old broken bones.
I slept deep, air sucked out of my lungs.

On the Outer Banks, folks would tie themselves
to trees in case the house floated away. Isabel
landed twelve miles east, crossed Core Sound,
hit Davis and Stacy at 110 with a wall of water
ten feet high, five feet deep in two hundred homes.

After flood tide receded, I went to help
scrub mud. By the road downeast were
refrigerators, mustard-plaid sofas, FEMA
numbers sprayed on trees, carpets ripped out
but mildew in floors and walls forever.

"Deflect, deflect," I'd said. But no place is safe.
Hurricanes go where they want. When I ask
for fear and pain and loss to steer clear,
the storm may hit my neighbor. I should ask
instead for grace to handle whatever happens.

Jimmy Buffett at Monticello

In first-flush light I follow a man I could like.
His birder eyes see so much more than mine:
A golden-crowned kinglet sings behind the green-
house. A downy woodpecker digs at the suet.
A sapsucker rings the sycamore with holes.

Dan gives bird song words: In the field
the meadowlark says, "Laziness will kill you."
The Carolina wren on the fence—"Teakettle teakettle."
When it flies, "cheeseburger cheeseburger."
I hear, "Weedeater weedeater video video."

House finch, classic titmouse, bluebird on the wire.
Fording, I balance across rocks carrying Dan's tripod.
As the sun rises, an eagle flies by a reddening maple.
On the way back, since he ignores me, I wade through—
better to get wet feet than slip and sprain an ankle.

Who Cooks for You?

I
In the old swamp forest, owls and hawks
ate snakes, snakes and turtles ate frogs,
frogs ate dragonflies who ate the bugs.
Thirty years ago the old lady who sold me
this land pointed, "Nobody can ever build
back there." But when the railroad ripped up
tracks the town turned down the right-of-way.
I asked the owner to sell me the strip of land
behind my house, wet a foot deep when
it rains. As sea level rises, trees with wet feet
act like sponges to keep Beaufort dry.

Instead, a man upstate bought ten acres
to build forty-two houses where owls
used to hoot in centuries-old live-oaks
before humans moved to this relict dune.

I called state regulators and the feds who said,
"We can't worry about ten acres when we're
trying to save ten thousand. Besides, '404'
permits don't apply; that creek doesn't connect
to the ocean anymore." I watched the smug
developer plow down trees with a bush-hog.

II
With "The Oaks" on the subdivision sign,
I thought venerable live-oaks would surely
be safe as open space, that he'd leave
the holy grove on the dry slight rise.
But the berm of the road severed half
the tree roots, auguring certain death.
Between trunks of dying trees he cut
branches thick as an elephant's thigh and
built houses a swan's wingspan apart.

Now mitigation ponds and drainage ditches
breed mosquitoes. When I hear the dread
swoosh-swoosh and smell dank poison,
I grab my dog, run inside and pull down
windows to escape the slow truck that
sprays Malathion to kill the mosquitoes,
the bugs that birds eat and the birds.

III
On ditched and filled wet-land a new house
three stories high now fills the north sky,
built on concrete slab that will sink and crack.
Bright lights on a cul-de-sac shine
all night into my once-dark backyard
where I used to watch shooting stars.

By the back fence I've planted *Arbor vitae*,
bald cypress, river birch that will grow
to block the glare. On a moonlit spring
night warm enough to open windows,
once a year I hear two owls calling, "Who
cooks for you? Who cooks for you all?

Walk Cheerfully Over the Earth

Walking the St. James Way is prayer
        I pull a fist of purple buds by the path
from hedges of rosemary and lavender
        and lift the scent to my nose
like cathedral incense

        Through squares of color I walk to think
and to stop thinking, pavement or shade—what's next,
        what's lost—job, love, or resilience,
eager for fields of yellow sunflowers
        lavender to the horizon

The combine cuts a swath through fields of wheat
        steep green and yellow, blue-green grain
In medieval hill villages
        with stone houses and blue doors
trucks spew diesel fumes on cobble streets

        Along the Canal du Midi, land between
between two rivers and seas, between ancient time
        and now—vapor pillars climb into the clouds
The yellow sign says, "Do not swim: water may
        rise quickly when the nuclear plant releases"

Fifteen thousand years ago humans painted animals
        in the caves at Pech-Merle and Lascaux
French pastures seem too tame too groomed
        Finally a farmer told me five years ago
Mad cow disease emptied all the fields

In heat and drought the harvest is early
Between rows of peas and leeks, melons and beans
Cuckoos at dawn, whippoorwills at dusk
step by step like pilgrims for a thousand years
on the sacred path to Compostela

I walk to be aware of light and air
not sore toes or the weight of my pack
hoping to find a bunk before nightfall
If I ever need direction,
sunflowers, *tournesols*, turn to the light

Crépuscule/ Crepuscular

1
Taut silver like mackerel skin, tide
slides out the creek. Smooth mauve
glow surrounds the horizon.

The stiff breeze all day has dropped
at dusk. A mile south surf still roars
on the front beach. The round full

moon is pale until the sky darkens.
East southeast the lighthouse
blinks on every fifteen seconds.

This moment of calm on the dock,
grateful for bright constellations,
I watch Venus emerge.

2
Wrens, cardinals, sparrows, blackbirds
spit out cheap wild seed in the yard.
After the hurricane's high water,

rats chew into heat ducts below
my floor, attracted to cracked corn.
At dark when rats start to move,

I catch them through heat-vent holes
in black plastic snap traps tied to
fishing line. They squeak one last minute

as I pull them up, small wharf
rats with long tails. New metal ducts
will cost four thousand dollars.

Tonglen in Stockbridge Bowl

All night I dream I suffocate
At yoga camp I have slept little
    for three weeks
on a top bunk in an airless corner
    I breathe in dark dread
but do not breathe out ease

    In the morning I run
    down the hill to the lake
        to wake from drowning
    The lifeguard on the shore
    rakes my footprints in the gravel
        In winter she says
    the frozen lake groans like whale song

The sun leans over my shoulder
    when I swim and the water is still
    I stretch to catch my shadow on the bottom
Weeds below me grow in shallows
    where the sun reaches
I float my toes above the mud
    squeamish about slime

    Springs gush up cold water
    that leaves my hair clean
        but smells of weeds
    for which I feel new affinity
      If anything reaches for the light
      it's water weeds
          rooted in muck
    stretching to the surface
      to bloom and seed

Circling the shore I swim along the edge
    of the drop-off between weeds
    and dark water
Light prisms rise from the depths
    Buoyant when I swim
      breathing in dark
      breathing out light
I'm not afraid to sink

If They Came Our Way

on my father's 100th birthday

Over an icy mountain in morning mist
a day after shearing Leonora's sheep,
I follow the route Lee's troops took
from the south. He came north to find
shoes for his boys and burn a railroad bridge.
After the battle, farmers could not plant
bloody fields for two years. The national park
protects this soil now from motels on the north.
From the south it's hard to tell where private
pastures stop and the battlefield begins.

No one else is out this early. There is nothing
to see in the damp distance of the Peach Orchard,
the Rose Farm. On low ground the mist thins
and lifts. Up close the Wheatfield doesn't look
different than it would have a hundred and
fifty years ago, though quiet and empty now.
From Little Round Top thick fog like
unwashed fleece obscures the landscape.

When the 15th Alabama charged the 20th Maine
who held this hill, July 2, 1863, William Oates
said, "Blood stood in puddles" on these rocks.
Joshua Chamberlain, a Bowdoin professor,
ordered "Bayonets." He later wrote, "We kill
only to resist killing." These were men he could
befriend "if they came our way in good will."

I don't much care who won at Gettysburg.
Fifty-one thousand men dead or wounded,
and the maimed soon dead from gangrene.
By the road, there's a view deeper into the woods
of stone walls, streambeds. Emerging from a cloud
like soldiers stumbling from the smoke, tall thin
saplings grow where the mowing stopped.

Green Thought in Green Shade

annihilating all that's made
Andrew Marvell

We have lost their laughing color in the sky,
the only wild parrot this far north,
lost because honeybees filled their nests,
because we chopped down cypress swamps.

I count seven askew in Audubon's print beside my bed:
life size, a foot long, leaf-green tail and wings,
yellow neck and scarlet cheeks, big black eyes
and curved beaks biting cockleburs.

When one bright parrot was shot:
the loud emerald flock would sink
and surround her, bewildered.
We humans rarely see such devotion.

Was it love? fearlessness or folly? For a hunter
could shoot a hundred more on the ground
and fill a burlap sack for the milliner
to adorn preening ladies' bonnets.

One gunman said, "Several shots fill a basket."
After shooting these seven to paint, Audubon
wrote: "The flesh is tolerable food. But,
kept as pets, they never learn to talk."

Shot for green fashion-feathers.
Shot because hundreds picked an orchard clean,
in fact bit to the core for the seeds
and spit out whole the white apple fruit.

The last died in the wild a hundred years ago.
The last one in a zoo soon after. What fun
would one have alone who
frolicked with such raucous company?

Women no longer wear feathered hats
but Carolina Parakeets are long gone
like the Ivory-Bill despite uncertain
flashes of vivid green through the trees.

Rowing Forward, Facing Backward

Spartina grass is new spring-green.
Mating season, red-wing blackbirds
claim territory on myrtle and yaupon
with sweet trills. Triplets of swallows
hover and dip. On stilts, great egrets
wade by oysters and red-billed
oyster-catchers on spreading sand flats
exposed at low tide.

I row the tidal creek, open at both ends
between Gallants Channel and white
phosphate domes at Morehead port.
Right here the state wants to sink
pilings in the marsh for a high bridge
to move tractor-trailer trucks faster
to the port. Small town, no rush,
I don't mind waiting for the
old drawbridge to open or close.

I skim over shallows, facing backward.
The sliding-seat shell I row draws scant
inches. In skinny water I float light and
fast. If I run aground, I won't step
out or I'd sink thigh deep into muck.
If I drag the boat, oyster shells would
lacerate my ankles and scrape the race-
slick hull. Instead, I can wait an hour
for the tide to rise, watching
a lone blue heron watch the water.

Acknowledgments

These poems appeared in the following publications:

"Green Thought in Green Shade" in *Literary Trails of Eastern North Carolina* (UNC Press, 2013)

"If They Came Our Way," 2012 Guy Owen Poetry Prize in *Southern Poetry Review*

"Rowing Forward, Facing Backward" in *Tar River Poetry*

"Salt Runs in My Blood" as "Chesapeake Homeplace" in *ISLE: Interdisciplinary Studies in Literature and Environment*

"Deep Pool" in *Kakalak 2008 Anthology of Carolina Poets*

"Sunbright Both Burn" in *The Land Report*

"Equilibrate" as "Submerged" in *Journey Proud, A Collection of Southern Women's Personal Writing*

Thanks for residencies at Virginia Center for the Creative Arts at Sweet Briar and Auvillar, France; Bread Loaf, Vermont Studio Center, and a Provincetown Dune Shack. And for fellowships from National Endowment for the Humanities, National Science Foundation, Fulbright, North Carolina Arts Council, American Association of University Women. I learned about craft from writers in workshops I took and taught. Gratitude to my Beaufort Writing Group critique community and to my Cape Cod cousins.

Reviews

Her eye for detail, her vision of the inner core of what she finds in Nature, her ideas as they come through imagery: **Susan Schmidt** can be a writer who matters. —Richard Krawiec

Susan Schmidt's poetry is tidal, seasonal, evolutionary. Traveling by wind, muscle, and memory from the Chesapeake to the Camino de Santiago, she sings like a Silkie with a human heart—about risk, loss, and resilience. Songs of her father are personal and epic. She sights birds near extinction or already lost. Her poems consider both her own fate and the planet. Schmidt writes a true line that skims, like her boat, over the surface of time and place.   —Sandy Morgan

Kakapo Press publishes place-based books.
The kākāpō is an endangered New Zealand parrot.

Photo of kākāpō by Sabine Bernert
Crown © Department of Conservation Te Papa Atawhai
http://kakaporecovery.org.nz/donate/

About the Author

As developmental editor, **SUSAN SCHMIDT** polishes science and history books, novels, and memoirs—with the same mindfulness as pruning apple trees. She has been a professor of literature and environmental decision-making, sailboat delivery captain, and government science-policy analyst. She has a doctorate in American literature and a Masters in Environmental Sciences.

To witness natural diversity, she walked the Camino de Santiago, Cornwall Coastal Path, Scottish Highlands, Ring of Kerry, and Appalachian Trail; surveyed birds in Kenya, Costa Rica, and Ecuador; paddled Prince William Sound and Milford Sound; and delivered sailboats to the West Indies. Her homeplace is the Chesapeake Bay in Virginia, and her homeport is Beaufort, North Carolina, where she walks beaches with her Boykin Spaniel.

Her poems won the 2012 Guy Owen Poetry Prize and appear in *Literary Trails of Eastern North Carolina*. She wrote *Landfall Along the Chesapeake, In the Wake of Captain John Smith*, an ecological history and boat adventure, and *Song of Moving Water*, an environmental novel about a young woman organizing an Appalachian community to oppose a dam.

susu@susanschmidt.net
www.susanschmidt.net

www.ingramcontent.com/pod-product-compliance
Lightning Source LLC
Chambersburg PA
CBHW022125280326
41933CB00007B/549